It's Too Dark In The Forest

By Darrell Lee

Table of Contents

Chapters

1. Breaking the rules

2. No one's looking anyway.

3. Hard to kill

4. One more chance

5. Friends

6. My Hero

7. It's a brand-new day.

8. I see the Light

The scriptures used are from the New International Bible and King James Bible.

Preface

This book came to me as I sat down and thought about how to accomplish this next move for my organization. I sometimes realized, **"It's too dark in the forest."**

In our attempts to progress, we can find ourselves in a momentary confusion where we cannot see the objectives.

Those are the times when things can be dark. When faced with those moments, we need to reflect on where we have been and the things we have gained victory over, so we can adequately categorize what we are facing.

Chapter One

Breaking The Rules

Here is an excellent question: Who said that breaking all the rules is always wrong?

Some rules are gravitated to make it impossible for you to win, so: What are you doing in that case?

Do you keep playing, knowing that the outcome will not be favorable, or do you decide to change the rules?

Who said I could not start my entrepreneurial endeavors because I may not hold a master's degree in Business Administration? Does that rule exist to help me or hinder me? Please understand me; I am not saying proper education is terrible. I'm simply saying that if that is not my quest, will I be somehow disqualified from success?

Throughout your life, you worked hard, and to be honest, you will get the best in life. Why are lazy people who don't put effort into anything but make out like a bandit?

Would you say someone breaking the rules or getting help from a friend is wrong?

Part of the reason for their success is that they had some help. In some cases, this may not follow the rules of the letter, but I am not saying they are cheating; you be the judge.

Is there a possibility that the influence that others may have is what provides aid to that slothful individual?

Chapter One

Breaking The Rules

Rules are all around us; they're in the laws that govern our life. They are in the jobs that we work for; they exist with the friends we have in our lives.

However, there are times in our lives when we cannot follow the rules that tell us to terminate someone's employment unjustifiably.
For nothing short of stupid reasons, they do not consider the outcome.

If you are in that position of authority, you get to decide who stays and who goes.
I employ you to honestly evaluate each situation and base your decision on what is right.

Sometimes what is right doesn't always look authoritative.

When we look at building a business, some very traditional laws are in place.

These laws state that you are to have an executive summary, and a good business can't start without a solid business plan.

We need finances, and we need to understand how the operation works and the brick, and mortar cost for the location. The list can go on and on, having no apparent end.

These are basic principles and rules for someone who wants to enter the business.

But is that all necessary in today's business climate? Can I develop my plan? Can I build my business? Can I achieve those things without becoming a victim of the process?

I present everything to the financial institutions and wait for people to approve or disapprove of what I intend to do. Is there another way?

Chapter One

Breaking The Rules

When I speak of breaking the rules, I am talking about finding ways to accomplish the things that need to get done to move to the next stage in life by using methods other than those that are traditional.

Who said you need an abundance of capital to start that business? Technology can initiate websites for free, and you can have company phone numbers for free. When you explore opportunities, you realize you can get your business up and off the ground for practically nothing. It depends on what type of business you are referencing.

So, don't fall for what I cannot find and accomplish because it goes against the rules. But sometimes, understanding authorities have to be broken.

We can take a page from the old days; if someone was building something and did not have adequate supplies or additional funding, they bartered for it. If I need computer skills, you have it; you need financial skills, I have it; it's a fair exchange, not robbery.

Let's look at what we need for our greatness and go about the process of breaking every rule we can fail.

But remember that even breaking the rules has rules; in this case, you must be honest and ethically correct.

Chapter One

Breaking The Rules

Lying to get ahead is nothing short of being deceitful and corruptive. When you use methods like that, you have no choice but to continue to do them to cover up the ones you have executed in the past.

This type of behavior can find you in a dark place, where you can no longer see the plan you originally had for your life and your business because it is poisoned and covered in corruption and deceit. Don't allow the things that you want to cause you to live in the forest; it is a place where the darkness hides many things.

As the sun rises, it breaks through the enchanted forest and reveals the sunlight, giving us a view of the clear and beautiful life beholds.

You need to move forward, look to break the rules, make positive changes, and help people grow and become the best they can be.

Remember to be honest and trustworthy, and enjoy yourself as you break the rules, sometimes designed to hold you back. Open up that new door of opportunity and march right through it with the handbook on Breaking Rules.

Chapter One

Breaking the rules

P.S.
I can recall when I decided that I no longer wanted to work in the management field in my industry. Instead, I decided to make a 360-degree turn and go into an area I did not know.

Now! the challenging part, I did not have the qualifications to be accepted, so I decided to make a plan that I believed would turn out in my favor.

I first needed to look at the plan, but I was on a financial budget, which meant I had to do it without becoming expensive but staying within my budget. I went to a consignment shop, where I purchased a blue pinstripe (Brooks Brothers) suit, a pair of slightly too-small wingtips; they made my feet hurt, a white shirt, and a red tie. The entire outfit cost me a whopping $60.

I then researched some of the best companies in the industry that I was looking to be a part of, and I successfully found one in my city. I arranged to see the recruiter; he scheduled the interview for two weeks. During that time, I went to the library daily and read all the information I could about the industry, which helped me know how the company works. In addition, I also want to understand the people that may be involved in my interview. On the interview day, I walked into the office as if I had been a businessman all my life.

The recruiter informed me they interviewed 50 individuals before picking the right one for their company. I responded, "no need to look further; I am that one." I secured the position and worked for several years before leaving. They paid for my education, additional license, and office space, and I grasped a strong understanding of the industry through collaboration.

Now, if you can recall what I said in the beginning, " I did not qualify, which means I did not follow the rules; I broke them."

If I had followed the rules of the letter, I would've never scheduled the interview, secured the position, and never experienced the opportunity. Sometimes, in life, governments are not in our favor.

Chapter One

Breaking The Rules

Jesus Broke the Rules

Jesus Heals a Crippled Woman on The Sabbath

On a Sabbath, Jesus taught in one of the synagogues, and a woman whose spirit had reduced her way of living because she had a disability for eighteen years was there.

She was bent over and could not straighten up at all.

When Jesus saw her, he called her forward and said, "Woman, you are set free from your infirmity."

Then he put his hands on her, and immediately she straightened up and praised God.

Indignant because Jesus had healed on the Sabbath, the synagogue leader said to the people, "There are six days for work. So come and be healed on those days, not on the Sabbath."

The Lord answered him, "You hypocrites! Doesn't each of you on the Sabbath untie your ox or donkey from the stall and lead it out to give it water?

Then should not this woman, a daughter of Abraham, whom Satan has kept bound for eighteen long years, be set free on the Sabbath day from what tied her?"

All his opponents were humiliated when he said this, but the people were delighted with his excellent work. Luke 13:10-17

Chapter Two

No One Is Looking, Anyway

Have you ever wanted to accomplish something so wrong so desperately that you were contemplating or maybe even willing to do something wrong?

And you say to yourself well, no one's looking anyway; no one would know how I did this or who it may have offended as long as I get it done. In my mind, that's all that matters. Have you ever asked yourself that, or have you ever actually done it?

It is not unusual or uncommon for people to have thoughts contradictory to their ethics and beliefs because sometimes things get tough. But, at those times, you must pull yourself out of that dark forest and see the light to accomplish greatness.

One thing we should keep in mind, just because we do not see someone looking does not mean they're not.

Sometimes, people look at you as a means to help you determine what you should do. After all, we don't know other people's situations, so even though we believe no one can see us doesn't mean that no one is looking or that no one has seen us.

Sometimes, in our life, things happen out of the sight of people as a test to see how we will handle them. Will we fall into temptation, or will we stand firm to our core values?

An old saying holds, "the things that are done in the dark always come to light."

Doing sneaky things and wrong can cause other things to manifest themselves in your life, and those things can keep you trapped in the dark forest of confusion for years to come.

Chapter Two

No One Is Looking, Anyway

I recall once when I found several money orders totaling around $4000. An individual told me that I should sign the money orders over to myself and cash them in, and do what I wanted to do with the money.

To be perfectly honest with you, I thought about it repeatedly; something that wasn't very helpful came to my mind. Who was looking anyway? No one would know if I took the money.

At that time, I was at a crossroads; I had to decide whether to cash in the money orders or return them to the institution as indicated in the document. I can tell you I didn't come up with a conclusion quickly. It took a couple of days of me staring at the money orders on the countertop before I finally decided that I was going to return them to the company indicated on the document.

There comes a time when you will have to make that decision to do what is right, and it may be uncomfortable.

Maybe you do not want to make the right decision; you can decide to answer your other side, but remember this, when you do not believe anyone may be looking, never lose sight of the fact that God is always looking. After all, God is Omnipresent.

He sees everything we do so, holds our standards high, and does not disregard them for moments when you think no one is watching because he is surprised someone's always watching.

Chapter Two

No One Is Looking, Anyway

Some trees grew in our area and looked like cigars when they changed from green to brown. When we felt no one was looking, my brother and I decided to pick Johnny Smokers; we chose them just to have fun.

On this particular day, we walked to where we picked the smokers; we would walk alongside the train tracks to get to the trees on the top of a hill. I remembered thinking I was going to get a lot of smokers today.

After we finished picking the smokers, it was getting late, so we decided it was time to go home. I looked at my brother's bucket; he had more smokers than I did. My comment to him was giving me some of those because you have more than me. He said, "no, you should have gotten more for yourself."

I tapped him again on the shoulder as we walked down the hill and asked him again. He turned around and said, "I already told you no." At that point, I looked around and saw no one was looking back at me.

Because there was no one around, I pushed him down the hill so I could take his smoke. My action cost them a terrible gash to his knee, and he began to bleed.

Chapter Two

No One Is Looking, Anyway

I was so scared my mother and father would punish me, so I told my brother to say he fell on his own, and his answer was "NO!".

My parents severely punished me for what I did.

While my brother went on to show his injury off to as many sympathetic girls as he could, he claimed he was hurt; oh, poor guy!

The day my brother saw what I did, so did God. I regret that moment whenever I see him in a pair of shorts.

We have to pay attention when our thoughts become conniving and sinister. We want to do wrong things to get what we think we should have, understanding that it's a dark forest.

If we allow greed and selfishness to grow in our lives, it will lead us down that road to the dark forest, where sometimes those things that we feel are not that big of a deal can turn out to be the disaster of a lifetime.

Do all you can to live a good life and display compassion for people, whether you know them, are related to them or have no connection whatsoever. And remember, someone's always looking when you think no one's looking.

Chapter Three

Hard To Kill

Have you ever heard someone say to you," old habits are hard to break"? Considering the psychological position habits take in our lives, they can be tough to kill.

Sometimes, you can be left in a dark place trying to see your way out because of old habits, businesses, and things.

The things that hold us down and fight against our progress in life can sometimes have a very subtle and quiet approach. It can sneak up on us, and before we know it overtakes us. When that happens in our life, we can find ourselves struggling to get out of something tough to kill.

People sometimes wrestle with problems and issues for years and still succumb to their situation. Because they haven't learned how to fight correctly, they become victims. Over time they can be surrounded by darkness, unable to see the beauty of the forest because it is simply too dark.

Many aspired life changes could lead someone into the wrong occupation and some into a health struggle they feel complied to act on. Others in the form of people that show you pleasantries simultaneously, hoping that you do not make it through, and quietly orchestrating your demise.

While being hard to kill can be something not so good, it could be a great thing, depending on how you look at it, instead of fighting with all your habits. The same old places and things sometimes realize they cannot harm you. Then you become hard to kill, and your dreams become a reality because you put up the fight necessary to win.

Chapter Three

Hard To Kill

When people try to kill you with their words and tell you what you can do and who you are not, take into account that you are looking at a stone-cold killer, and on this day, you will not be their victim.

In doing that, we assure you that nothing will stop you from succeeding, especially those who want to see your dreams and aspirations assassinated.

Do you know who the assassins are in your life? The naysayers, as the old saying goes, "smile in your face, but stab you in the back." Keep this in mind; these types can only function when you give them space in your life to have that level of effect on you.

A target that is not in motion is always easier to hit than one that is in constant movement staying on track with your intended destiny, making it hard for others to hold you back, and you become hard to kill.

If you hold onto the attitude of a winner, you will always look for a way of escape when you are under attack. Keep fighting and continue to move in the direction of the light.

Chapter Three

Hard To Kill

Life can hit you so hard sometimes that you bleed internally because no one can see it; you act like all is well.

There is an old saying, "fake it till you make it" in some cases, it says you will make it. Some things can be so complex that you do not have the answer. Some items can be so dark that you cannot find your way. This could mean that sometimes, faking it until you make it because you don't know if you made it or are faking it, right? And when that day comes, just keep moving; remember, a target in motion is more challenging to hit than one still.

I remember when my father passed away, and everyone was crying and emotional, but I was not. I displayed no emotions at all. I walked around as if everything was just fine. Later on, I looked back and realized I was faking it all. I hid my emotions; I did not want to deal with the outcome.

One day in church on Father's Day, 16 years later, I lost the ability to fake it any further, fell to the ground weeping, and cried over the loss of my father 16 years earlier. That was a heavy weight to carry for such a long time.

Sometimes the darkness in the forest is created through ourselves; we need to address those things that can keep us in the dark. When you do not release your emotions, you suffer needlessly.

Chapter Four

One More Chance

Opportunity

There is an old saying: Don't throw out the baby with the bathwater.

Sometimes we just need one more chance, another opportunity to get things right when we mess up. People are not always willing to give folks another chance at something as if they've never done anything wrong themselves. When your time comes around, you need to consider it before you refuse someone. Sometimes give them another opportunity to get something correct. You need to look at it; somewhere along the way, you were given another opportunity somewhere along the way.

It reminds me of one of the reasons why I like sports so much. Joining a team will give you many chances to get things right, from tryouts to make the team. It doesn't matter what a particular skill set is; it is essential to understand what it means to get one chance to make the squad.

Sometimes, things can seem very dark when you do not have another chance to get them right—making you feel like you could be more successful.

You must remember that second chances and opportunities don't always come around again in the same way.

So, you have to put your very best foot forward. You must convince those who can give you a chance that you deserve it.

There is no time to walk around with your head hung down, feeling sorry for yourself because you did not make it the first time. It is time to reevaluate your approach, know what you've done incorrectly, make adjustments, and capture your second chance.

Chapter Four

One More Chance

Sometimes, we are told what we shouldn't do, but because it comes from people we know and associate with, we discount it and believe it will not work; after all, they only told me that because you're a friend of mine.

At those times, we can miss out on opportunities because we need to dig past the surface to see if what is being said is legitimate. We need to realize sometimes that just because someone knows us does not mean that their response to our situations is strictly emotional. It can come from a place of wisdom if we listen; when we do hear, we can apply what is reasonable and reject what is not.

Sometimes, we can create our forest and not see what has happened because we are in the woods.

Talk to me

Second chances, in some cases, can be challenging; people can be impacted so severely that they are unwilling to offer you another opportunity to do the same thing. Therefore, they choose to disconnect and not allow you any chance to cause them to be damaged again, just like it can happen to any individual, and the same can happen in your case. You can feel the same way about someone; you can believe that that individual does not deserve another chance and close the door on them for a very long time.

It reminds me of a time when my grandmother and mother disconnected over some issues; I was too young to understand, but I wasn't too young to take sides. At that moment, I aligned myself with my mother and made a conscious decision that I would never again visit my grandmother.

So, I disconnected myself from all my family members on my father's side and refused to give anyone another chance. I said the only time I would speak with my grandmother again or see her was when she was on her deathbed. Unfortunately, that statement came true.

Chapter Four

One More Chance

When I was asked to visit my grandmother in the hospital, I refused, still holding onto my unwillingness to speak with her again due to the pain and heartache she caused my mother. My mother convinced me to go and see her; when I arrived, she said she was happy to see me and wanted to tell me how sorry she was about how things went with her and my mother; she asked me to forgive her.

That was the first time I had spoken with her in many years. I realized then that it was just as many years that I had not spoken with anyone in my family on my father's side. It's incredible how much time can get away from you, incredibly when angry. I decided at that moment that I wasn't as mad as I thought, and I have my mother to thank for opening my eyes to something because she forgave her years ago. She offered me one more chance long ago, and now it was my turn.

Refusal to allow individuals to have one more chance is another way to keep them on the dark side of the forest.

It doesn't matter who you are if you are unwilling to give someone else another chance. This can have devastating results on your life as well as those who will impact you.

For years even our planet has been telling us to make corrections that will allow us to have one more chance to repair things like climate change that we now see all over the globe. In many cases, we have failed to respond and refuse to give our planet another chance at recovery.

But on the other hand, when we allow for another chance, we open the door to hope, restoration, and worth, and these things help to balance my life and our planet.

Jesus came to this world to offer us all one more chance and to offer his life. We can all see how important it is to forget it, release people of offenses, and present them with one more option. Understand me; this doesn't mean someone offends you; you can say it's "OK." Let's be buddy buddies, but it does mean that you are willing to offer them another opportunity to correct those mistakes, even if you do not continue the friendship at the level it once was.

Chapter Five

Friends

What exactly does that mean to be someone's friend? Let's look at it to identify how many friends we have. It will also help us to see if we are a friend to someone that is a real friend.

People often are quick to say this person is my friend on social media, along with my other 500 friends but really, how many of these people do you know? We get into disagreements and arguments over social media then leads to people not liking people, but how can it be when you don't even know?

One of the reasons is social media has created such a dark black forest that often time you have no idea or concept of the person you're communicating to all the other end but yet you hold these long, intense, detailed conversations that give them nothing but information about the future before it's all said and done they can knock on your front door because they know exactly where you live after they one of your 500 friends.

The times we live in now have a dark forest that sometimes is strategically placed in our lives to prevent us from reaching destiny. Unfortunately, you could spin your entire life seeing nothing because what you need to see is blocked by the forest of a supposed friend.

Well, if you have one individual in your life that you can call your friend who can not see you for years and suddenly see you and pick up exactly where you left off. Who will walk you through difficult times and celebrate in your good times, offer words of wisdom and friendship, and never judge you based on others' opinions; then I'll say you are a fortunate individual.

Chapter Five

Friends

Just because you call yourself someone's friend, and you declare them to be yours, does not necessarily mean that their friendship goes beyond the statement, "the best way to know if someone is the true friend is by their actions when you are in a situation." Sometimes that individual does not consider themselves a friend. They may believe that you are just some person that they know. In that case, did they lie, or did you misunderstand the relationship?

Those issues can be avoided by clearly recognizing the individual's position and yourself.

You can avoid those dark moments of hurt feelings and confusion by having clarity through communication. You won't know exactly where you stand.

Chapter Six

My Hero

You need to have at least one hero in your life. That individual that, through thick and thin; good times and bad times; and in different times; has never changed their position about you and is always ready to come to your rescue. I want to take this moment to talk about two people in my life who have been my heroes. And without them, my situation could've turned out quite differently.

The first person I would like to tell you about is my mother, Margaret Lee. I have yet to find another individual so brave and determined. My father, John Sr. taught me discipline; my mother taught me compassion, understanding, and patience. She was an absolute believer in the fact that it would always get better. Though I couldn't understand it because what we were looking at was the reality of the situation because it did not dictate any signs of getting better.

My father was a Deacon in the church, and my mother was a member of the Nurse's Unit. My mother loved the church more than my father did.

When my big brother John Jr. passed away, my mother said to my father, "let's go to church."

My little brother Keith passed away; my mother said to my father ``let's go to church".

My two twin sisters passed away; my mother said to my father, "let's go to church!'.

And when my little sister Tammytha, the heart of my heart, passed away, my mother said," let's go to church."

I lost five siblings, but my mother lost five of her children, and through it all, my mother still raised my siblings and me, the grandchildren, and great-grandchildren. How she did it still amazes me. I still cannot comprehend or understand how she did it all.

She kept the family safe and together until she went home to be with the Lord.

WE CAN FIND LIGHT THROUGH DARKNESS IF WE KEEP LOOKING.

Chapter Six

My Hero

My second hero is my little sister Tammytha, whom I call my Little-Big sister because she had so much wisdom and bravery.

She had some physical challenges, and later we discovered that she also had some learning challenges, but through it all, she never wanted to stop asking me to teach her something new.

Tammytha loved martial arts, so I made a uniform that would fit her, and we would practice every day. She would show me that she could make new moves, and I would teach her more.

As she got a little older, she had several surgeries because of a hole in her heart, and she needed a pacemaker. After every surgery, she would always smile and be happy. She would ask me again, in her words, "to teach me something new."

Tammthya loved life and was grateful for it, and she robbed me of the right to complain about anything because I was healthy. What if I had a headache one day or a stomach ache, I felt I had no reason to complain.

I didn't have nearly the issues she did, and Tammytha never complained; therefore, I couldn't complain either. She was my hero.

Tammytha was called home to heaven at the age of 11 years old. Ultimately, she taught me how to stand up and be a man. She did not allow those dark moments of not feeling well to take from her happiness; it was never too dark in the forest for her, My Hero.

Chapter Seven

It's a Brand-New Day

You know, one of the most beautiful things we get to experience is a brand-new day. We welcome the chance to look at things in a brand new way, face unique challenges, and overcome obstacles in the beauty of another day.

One thing is sure about a day: we all must learn to use it to the highest point of success and accomplishment we possibly can. There's something else about a brand new day. We are not guaranteed to see one. The only thing we can guarantee is that it will all end someday for us.

A recent report shows Americans watch about four or five hours of television daily for about 77 days a year; that's a little over 35 hours a week. It's like a second job; what a waste of a day.

Do you know the other exciting thing about a day is anywhere from 8 to 10 hours of a day is spent with coworkers, and in some cases, they are total strangers? How do you spend more time within a day, at least busy, than with your family on the same day? So, you need to treat those moments like a brand new day, every day.

Don't allow a portion of a day to destroy the balance of the day; learn how to see through the forest of things that come to you every day to disrupt you. Confusion makes you feel as if there's no sense in going on because to pay attention to those things and to give credit and energy to those things is to cause indefinite blindness. This is the type of blindness that exists in people who have the vision to see. Choose to remain in the darkness by allowing the entire day to be consumed with issues, and they drag those issues home with them and, in many cases, deposit them into their families.

Chapter Seven

It's a Brand-New Day

It is a brand new day when you can open your eyes, look to the heavens, and say thank you, Jesus, for another day. You need to get into the habit of realizing that it is not just another day, but it's a brand-new day that you've never seen before. One that has never existed, but here it is now, a brand-new tremendous, and wonderful day.

Look at it, and decide what you want to accomplish on this day. This may be the day you finally make that move toward your business or apply for the promotion. In any case, you are facing new opportunities, unlike before, because this new day is unlike any day before. Look at this day through clear eyes, and we will see all God has for us.

God can change your life in one day, all the troubles you could be experiencing can be gone in the blink of an eye, and everything can be new. Sometimes, to share that, you have to believe that God will make it available for you, and when you think that, you can hold on, as the old folks say, just a bit longer.

Some people don't believe those good things can consistently happen to them, and as a result, they look for everything that could be wrong in the day and then wonder why things are just not working out for them. Sometimes, you must take your eyes off all your situations and place them on the truth and the living God with all power in His hands.

As we live in these difficult times, we'll all have to embrace every day. We have to look at our lives in a way we can appreciate every day because one thing is for sure, two things for certain you are not promised tomorrow.

Chapter Eight

I See The Light

Sometimes life can present some very complicated issues and confusing moments that can cause things to look impossible and give you a dismal look at what tomorrow brings you. I can understand it because if you live long enough, you will experience some of those moments; they can come in many ways.

It could result from a wrong diagnosis from your doctor or an unfavorable financial position that can confuse you about what tomorrow brings. It could be an inconvenient situation in the family, an argument that could separate siblings, and present some very dark times. This is when you are lost in the forest and need clarification about your next step.

The point where you need to recognize that you have very little control over your life is when you understand just how small you are in the grand scheme of things. You have to begin to ask the right questions about your position in life and how to walk out this life the way God has intended for you instead of experiencing the emptiness and lack that comes from no relationship and a life without joy.

The Bible says, "weeping may endure for a night, but joy comes in the morning." you have to begin to ask yourself, what does my joy look like, and what will bring my morning back? Keep in mind that light and dark cannot exist in the same space at the same time together; one must go.

Darkness creates difficulty, possibly leaving you guessing if you're going in the right direction. It will continue to do that as long as you remain in the dark.

In many cases, people are in the dark about their lives, and what is even more devastating. Darkness, in some cases, has existed for a very long time, and if they are not determined to discover the light in a situation, then darkness will always remain prevalent.

However, the beautiful thing is that your vision becomes clear and attainable when you click on the light switch or when the sun rises. You no longer need assistance to reach your destination because you see the morning, and with the light comes second chances.

Chapter Eight

See The Light

Sometimes the desire to achieve in life doesn't allow us to see the dark side of other people or, in many cases, the dark side of ourselves. We can close our eyes to the reality that some things do not mean any good.

We can find ourselves in the middle of the forest, not even realizing how deep we've traveled. At this point, we may not be able to see our destination because the very thing we are chasing after has contributed to our loss of care and compassion, and our vision has become distorted.

By taking the path toward the light, I can reclaim those things lost due to the darkness. Those beautiful things give our life renewed meaning and bring us back in focus with all that we are and are meant to be.

The Forest can only remain dark for us if we decide not to come out of it, but if we keep moving forward, pressing for the mark, we can make it.

Therefore I will commit myself to the constant push toward greatness. I see the light and everything it encompasses, and it is a beautiful reach for the things in life that bring light and clarity to your existence. As long as you remain in touch with those things, you will always come through to the light.

From The Author

No matter your station in life, you must strive to do good and positively serve humanity.

Always keep in mind that situations in life will do two things. First, it will come; secondly, at some point, it will go. It knows you cannot allow something to keep you in a dark place for a prolonged period.

You will have to learn how to turn the light back on in a dark situation to discover the solutions that will take you to your next stage in life. Therefore when it gets dark in that forest, do not be concerned. Simply turn on your light and overcome your dark moment.

Made in the USA
Middletown, DE
08 March 2023

26389841R00018